You will come out on the other side

Have Confidence *in God*

STEPHANIE WOOLARD

BLUEPRINT PRESS
INTERNATIONALE

ISBN
978-1-959365-96-9 (Paperback)
978-1-959365-97-6 (eBook)
978-1-959365-95-2 (Hardcover)

Have
Confidence
in God

Table of Contents

Bragging about My God

Great is his name
that comes from above.
Always share
his wonderful love.
Never take him
for granted
in what he does.
My God is my savior,
and I love him too.

God Directed My Path

You took me by my hand.
You guide me well,
my friend.

You did it all for me
and gave me the victory.

Now I know with you
I can do all things.

I'm standing here
with a smile on my face
because I just ran
a wonderful race.

The devil tried
to keep me down
but God gave
me another round.

God Revealed Me

I never knew
I had another side
until one day
God let it rise.

I couldn't understand
why he chose me,
but he knew
before I was conceived.

God is the outcome
of this all.
He said, My child,
I will not let
you fall.

If I gave you
the gifts
to do my will,
I promise you, my child,
you will not be
shifted.

Haters Never Win

When you see a smile on my face,
don't you dare get disgraced.

Hear the sweetness in my voice?
Don't you dare raise your voice.

If you want to be my friend,
don't backstab me at the end.

Hater haters never win.

You see my light shining all day,
but it's not me—
it's God's way.

I ask the Lord to save my soul.

Why you hated,
I don't know.

Hater haters never win.

Hater haters never win.

Stephanie Woolard

Has God Ever Promised You Something?

*Whenever a storm
comes into your life,
don't give it death,
but give it life.
God's promise should
always stay with you
no matter what
you are going through.*

*The test may seem long,
but if you hold on,
God will bless you
with the love that belongs.*

Is She the One for Me?

I see you
staring at me,
praying to the Lord,
Is she the one
for me?

You watch me
so far away,
saying to the Lord,
Will I meet her
one day?

I will wait
for you, Lord,
to give me the sign,
praying you will
say yes
and she will
be mine.

Left Alone

I'm sitting here
all by myself,
wondering why I was left.
My friends, they were
all married and had help.
I still couldn't figure out
why I was left.

My prayer went out to the Lord,
seeking his face forever more.
He told me not to worry,
that I was in the process of learning.

I know you want to be married,
but I'm molding you to be
the person I want you to be.
That's the reason why
you're left alone
until I set you free.

Live and Not Die

It is not my time
to die.
Let me tell you the
reason why.
God created me
in his image
and gave me
life to finish.

He chose me
to do his
will.
Now I have to
do my part
and fulfill
what is real.

Stephanie Woolard

Poem

I watch you throughout the day,
mourning and crying away.
I can never know
what your pain feels like.
Only God knows what is right.
My heart is here for you,
but only God can bring
you through.

The Calling of My Life

*The calling of my life
means a lot to me.
If it wasn't for the
Lord on my side,
I wouldn't be able to see.
He gives me wisdom
in all that I do.
He orders my footsteps
and guides me too.*

*If you don't accept
my life through,
get thee behind me, Satan.
You have no clue.*

The Story of My Life

Don't let the devil
steal your story
when God gives
you the glory
for the victories.

I know the devil
may come your way,
but he doesn't
have the last say.

Trusting in God
will give you the
strength.
Stay with him
and you will
win it.

Trusting Jesus with My Secret

I had a secret
within my soul.
I couldn't tell
anyone because
it was old.
I knew I
could trust Jesus
with all my might,
praying that he would
show me the light.

Jesus said,
I will wipe
the tears
from your face,
give you the power and
the grace.
That secret that
you kept within,
I promise you now,
it will
be erased.

Stephanie Woolard

Well Done

It's me,
it's me, oh Lord.
I'm waiting here
at your door.
The Lord said,
Come on in.
I have called you
in the highest
place to stay,
where you will spend
your eternal life.

I must say,
no more worries,
no more pain.
My angels are here
to entertain.
The Lord said,
You have made
it to the kingdom come.
My child, your reward
is for work well done.

The Angels of Healing

Angels are in heaven
waiting to fly.
Angels are in heaven
to glorify.
God, send them down
to do your will.
There's people on earth
who need to be healed.

Deliver them all
from sickness and pain.
Give them confidence
and bless thy
holy name.

Stephanie Woolard

Power

Power is not easy
when you go through
the pain,
but even through
stormy weather,
it sometimes
rains.

The storm may rumble
up in the sky,
but angels are in heaven
waiting to fly.
God, send them down
to minister to me.
My arms are open wide—
I welcome thee.

Jesus, I Love You

Jesus, I love you dear
because you are sincere.
I can't make it through my day
unless you are here.
I feel you close.
Your burning sensation
is my inspiration.
I hear your voice
speaking out to me,
giving me the power
and the victory.

You are my shepherd,
and I am your sheep.
I'll glorify
your name
and proclaim
your will to be.

Stephanie Woolard

Thinking about You, My Love

I feel your heart beat
so far away.
Wishing you were close,
I must say,
I think about you
throughout each and every day.
Hoping these feelings will
go away,
I ask the Lord,
Is this real,
or is this something
that needs to be revealed?

I try to put these feelings
in the back of my head,
telling myself to go ahead;
the man whom you have
in mind
might not be for you
at this time.

Haters in the Church

I see you looking
with your fake smile,
but in your head
you are saying, Wow,
can't stay focused
on the service,
trying to figure
out everyone else's
worries.

You see me
giving God the praise,
and you have the
nerve to cross
your legs,
but at the end
of my shout,
I don't care
what my haters
think about.

Stephanie Woolard

Follow Jesus

You never walk alone
while Jesus is on the throne.
He will guide your footsteps every day.
He will lead you in the path of righteousness.
God said, I will never leave you
nor forsake you.
All I'm doing
through the test and trial,
I'm making you
so I can be proud.

Dreaming

A dream is
not a dream
unless at
the end
you can feel a pinch
after waking up.
You have to believe
the dream is
real, and
you have to survive
what was strife
in your life.

A Mother-and-Daughter Relationship

*It's a shame
when mother and daughter
have a fight
over the small
things they
could easily make right.*

*Mothers should always
protect their daughters.
Daughters should always
honor their mothers.*

*Never give anyone
or anything
a place in between.
Stay close in
your relationship;
say what you mean.*

Be Yourself

I wonder why you want
to wear other people's shoes,
not knowing
where they have been
and what they've been through.
You said, I want to be
like you,
but can you bear the pain
and grief
that I have to meet?

God made shoes for
everyone's feet.
Wear your own
and be victorious
in the race you have to beat.

Stephanie Woolard

Do Not Touch My Anointed Ones

You tried to kill
my spirit
with your lame lyric.
You tried to bring
me down,
wishing I wouldn't
come around.
God said,
Touch not my child,
but you disagree.

You kept hatin'
on me and
wouldn't let it be.
You know God's
Word is true.
Now the consequence
is meant for you.

Get Well Soon

You know when your
body is aching and
you are not faking,
we need our family
and friends to keep
us spiritually wakened.

Stephanie Woolard

The Angels of Miracles

Miracles do happen.
Miracles are true.
I know it can happen
if I believe in you.
God, I feel your holy power,
and it's working for me.
I will not give up
until you deliver me.
Deliver me from
all evil and pain.
I'm waiting to be
healed in Jesus's name.

The Spirit Man

I talked to you
through the spirit man.
I prayed that you would
understand.
Don't take this power
into your own hands.
It belongs to Jesus, and that's
his command.

Who Am I to Judge You?

I looked on the outside
of you,
thinking I knew you,
but looking through
a window
may give me the wrong clue.
I call you so many things,
not knowing you by your name.
I tried to judge you
before you even knew.

I have a question
to ask you:
Will you please give me
another chance?
I promise you this time
I will not judge you
by your pants.

Loving On You, Lord

What I love about
you, Lord,
is when you wrap
your arms around
me tight,
minister to me that
everything is all right.
Pour your blessings
down on me, Lord.
The angels that you send
I do adore.

Stephanie Woolard

You Can Go Higher

God can take you higher
where you've never been before.
God can take you higher
where the devil cannot go.
The things he does for me
I can't explain,
but I know what level
he takes me to;
there I will remain.

Don't Miss Your Angel

*When God sends an angel
into your life,
don't turn your head
thinking this can't be right.
He sent them out
to save your soul,
give you enough power,
and make you whole.*

*Know the signs
God reveals to you
and pray that
your angel will
see you through.*

Stephanie Woolard